TANDOOR & DRY DISHES

Contents

D0450191

*T*he tandoor is a traditional clay oven fired by charcoal and the wood of specific trees to give the food cooked in it a smoky flavor. Tandoori food, which uses very little fat, for there is hardly any frying or roasting involved, is still very tasty because the meat or vegetables are usually marinaded in spices and yoghurt to give them a succulent tenderness. Many leavened and unleavened breads are also made in the tandoor. A traditional clay tandoor can be got from a potter though electric and gas tandoors are also available in the market. All the recipes in this section, however, will work equally well with the oven and grill. The other dishes can be made, as usual, in the kadhai or griddle.

SERVES: 4

TANDOORI CHICKEN

The most popular barbecue chicken, a favorite all over the subcontinent.

Ingredients

Chicken, skinned, whole	2½ lb/2 birds	Oil for brushing	
Cream	3.5 fl oz/7 tbs	Orange color	1 drop
Cumin powder	¼ oz/1 tsp	Red chilli powder	¼ oz/1 tsp
Garlic paste	½ oz/1 tbs	Saffron	a pinch
Ginger paste	½ oz/1 tbs	Salt to taste	
Lemon juice	2 fl oz/4 tbs	Yoghurt	3.5 oz/7 tbs

Method

1. With a sharp knife make deep cuts on the breast, thigh and legs of the chicken.

2. Make a paste of lemon juice, red chilli powder and salt and rub over chicken. Set aside for 10 minutes.

3. Whip yoghurt. Add cream, ginger and garlic pastes, cumin, saffron and the orange color. Rub chicken with this mixture and keep aside for 3½ hours.

4. Skewer chicken through neck to tail and roast in a moderately hot oven for 8 minutes and then at 350 °F for 10 minutes.

5. Remove from oven. Hang skewers for 5-7 minutes to let moisture drip off.

6. Baste with oil and roast for a further 5 minutes.

Time
Preparation: 4 hours
Cooking: 20 minutes

To Serve
Cut into pieces and serve as a snack with onion rings and lemon wedges or as part of the main course

CHICKEN KHURCHAN

Shredded tandoori chicken stir-fried and flavored with real Indian spices.

Ingredients

Tandoori chicken	1	Green chilli, slit	1
Chaat masala	¼ oz/1 tsp	Lemon juice	½ fl oz/1 tbs
Coriander leaves, chopped	¼ oz/1 tsp	Onion rings	2 oz/¼ cup
Cooking oil	a few drops	Red chilli powder	a pinch
Garam masala	a pinch	Salt to taste	
Ginger-garlic paste	¼ oz/1 tsp	Tomatoes, chopped	1 oz/6 tsp
Ginger juliennes	¼ oz/1 tsp		

Method

1. Shred the tandoori chicken. In a frying pan heat the oil and sauté onion rings.

2. Add ginger-garlic paste and slit green chilli. Add the shredded chicken, salt, chaat masala, red chilli powder, garam masala and chopped coriander.

3. Stir-fry on medium flame.

4. Add lemon juice and chopped tomatoes. Fry for a few more minutes.

Time
Preparation: 20 minutes plus time to roast the chicken, if tandoori chicken is not available (for recipe see p. 3)
Cooking: 10 minutes

To Serve
Garnish with ginger juliennes and serve hot with any Indian bread and fresh salad

CHICKEN MALAI KEBAB

These smooth, creamy chicken kebabs are mildly flavored with cheddar cheese.

Ingredients

Boneless chicken cubes	2 lb	Ginger paste	1½ oz/3 tbs
Cheddar cheese, grated	2 oz/¼ cup	Green chillies, chopped fine	8
Coriander leaves, chopped	¾ oz/4 tsp	Mace (*javitri*) powder	⅛ oz/½ tsp
Cornstarch	½ oz/1 tbs	Nutmeg (*jaiphal*) powder	⅛ oz/½ tsp
Cream	4 fl oz/½ cup	Oil for basting	
Egg	1	Salt to taste	
Garlic paste	1¼ oz/7 tsp	White pepper powder	¼ oz/1 tsp

Method

1. Mix the ginger and garlic pastes, white pepper powder and salt. Rub mixture onto the chicken pieces. Set aside for 15 minutes.
2. Beat together egg, cheese, green chillies, coriander, cream, mace, nutmeg and cornstarch and rub chicken pieces with the mixture. Keep aside for 3 hours.

3. String together chicken pieces on a skewer an inch apart. Roast on a charcoal grill for 5 minutes or in a preheated oven at 275 °F for 7 minutes.
4. Remove. Hang skewers for 5-7 minutes to let excess moisture drip off. Brush with oil and roast again for 3 minutes.

Time
Preparation: 3½ hours
Cooking: 15 minutes

To Serve
Serve as a cocktail snack or as an accompaniment with the main course

JOOJHE-POTLI

This dish has chicken pieces roasted with spices in a bag of its own skin.

Ingredients

Chicken	2.2 lb	Mint leaves, chopped	1 oz/2 tbs
Black cumin		Processed cheese, grated	1½ oz/3 tbs
(*shah jeera*) seeds	⅛ oz/½ tsp	Salt to taste	
Chaat masala	⅛ oz/½ tsp	Red chilli powder	¼ oz/1 tsp
Coriander leaves, chopped	2 oz/¼ cup	Yoghurt	1½ oz/3 tbs
Cream	4 fl oz/½ cup		
Garam masala	¼ oz/1 tsp	**For salad**	
Garlic paste	1½ oz/3 tbs	Cucumber, sliced	½ lb
Ginger paste	1½ oz/3 tbs	Onion rings	1 lb
Groundnut/peanut oil	2½ fl oz/5 tbs	Tomatoes, sliced	½ lb
Lemon juice	2 fl oz/4 tbs		

Method

1. Cut chicken into 1inch cubes. Save skin.
2. Mix together salt, ginger and garlic pastes, lemon juice, red chilli powder, yoghurt and oil. Marinate chicken in this mixture for an hour. Rub chicken skin with salt and a pinch of red chilli powder.
3. Skewer chicken pieces and cook in a tandoor till half done, about 10 to 12 minutes. Remove from skewer.

4. Mix onions, ginger, coriander, grated cheese, fresh mint and cream with the half-cooked chicken. Fill the chicken pieces in the chicken skin and tie the ends with thread.
5. Skewer and cook in a tandoor till the skin turns brown in color or roast in a preheated oven at 275 °F till skin turns brown.
6. Remove thread and cut bag into half.

Time
Preparation: 1 hour
Cooking: 30 minutes

To Serve
Garnish with garam masala and chaat masala.•Arrange salad along the sides and serve hot

SERVES: 4

RESHMI KEBAB

An extra smooth chicken mince kebab rolled along the length of the skewer.

Ingredients

Chicken mince/ground	2.2 lb		Ginger, finely chopped	1 oz/2 tbs
Cashew nuts, pounded	2 oz/¼ cup		Oil for basting	
Cooking oil	¾ fl oz/4 tsp		Onions, chopped	¾ oz/4 tsp
Coriander leaves, chopped	¾ oz/4 tsp		Salt to taste	
Cumin (*jeera*) powder	½ oz/1 tbs		White butter for brushing	
Eggs	2		White pepper powder	¼ oz/1 tsp
Garam masala	¼ oz/1 tsp		Red chilli powder	¼ oz/1 tsp

Method

1. Whip the eggs, add cumin, red chilli powder, white pepper powder and oil. Add to the ground chicken and mix well. Set aside for 10 minutes.

2. Add cashewnuts, ginger, onions, coriander and garam masala. Mix well. Divide into 10 equal portions.

3. Wrap two portions along each skewer

using wet hands. Keep 2 inches between each portion. Like this prepare five skewers.

4. Roast in a moderately hot tandoor or charcoal grill till till golden brown, about 6 minutes or roast in a preheated oven at 300 °F for 8 minutes. Baste once with oil. Remove from skewers and brush with white butter.

Tip

Time
Preparation: 30 minutes
Cooking: 6 minutes

To Serve
Serve with onion rings and lemon wedges

CHICKEN TIKKA

Boneless chicken chunks roasted with spices make a delicious cocktail snack.

Ingredients

Chicken, deboned	2 lb	Mace (*javitri*) powder	⅛ oz/½ tsp
Cooking oil	2 fl oz/4 tbs	Oil for basting	
Cumin (*jeera*) powder	⅛ oz/½ tsp	Red chilli powder	¼ oz/1 tsp
Garlic paste	1½ oz/3 tbs	Salt to taste	
Ginger paste	1½ oz/3 tbs	Turmeric powder	⅛ oz/½ tsp
Gram flour (*besan*)	¾ oz/4 tsp	White pepper	
Green cardamom powder	⅛ oz/½ tsp	powder	⅛ oz/½ tsp
Lemon juice	2 fl oz/4 tbs	Yoghurt	1½ oz/3 tbs

Method

1. Cut chicken into 1 inch cubes.
2. Whip yoghurt and mix in all other ingredients. Marinate chicken pieces in it and keep aside for 3 hours.
3. Skewer each piece an inch apart and roast in a tandoor for 3 minutes.
4. Brush with oil and roast again in a preheated oven at 350 °F for 10 minutes, basting at least twice.

Time
Preparation: 3½ hours
Cooking: 10 minutes

To Serve
Remove to a platter and serve with onion rings and mint chutney

CHICKEN SOOLA

A hearty Rajasthani delicacy, this chicken barbecue evokes images of grand sand dunes, roaring camp fires and lilting folk music.

Ingredients

Chicken, leg and breast pieces	1 lb
Almond paste	1/4 oz/1 tsp
Cooking oil or	
Clarified butter (*ghee*)	2 fl oz/4 tbs
Garlic paste, browned	1/4 oz/1 tsp
Ginger paste	1/4 oz/1 tsp
Khoya, grated	1 oz/5 tsp
Onion paste, browned	2 oz/1/4 cup
Raw papaya paste	4 oz/1/2 cup
Red chilli powder	1/4 oz/1 tsp
Roasted gram, powdered	1/8 oz/1/2 tsp
Salt to taste	
Yoghurt	1/4 oz/1 tsp

Method

1. Clean and dry chicken pieces and prick all over with a fork. Marinate with raw papaya and set aside for 12 hours or overnight.
2. Remove papaya paste and discard. Do not wash chicken.
3. Mix together all ingredients except cooking oil and marinate chicken in it.
4. Skewer pieces close together, levelling the mixture from top to bottom. Wrap a string tautly along skewered chicken to keep the pieces firm while cooking.
5. Burn charcoal in the barbecue or grill till white ash appears on the surface and cook, keeping chicken pieces 6 inches above the fire.
6. Cook on low fire till chicken is tender, then stroke fire to medium heat, baste chicken with a little oil at a time, till all the oil is over and the chicken is well browned. Alternatively, the chicken can be cooked in a preheated oven at 275 °F for 15 minutes.

Time	**To serve**
Preparation: Overnight + 1½ hours	Remove string and serve hot with mint
Cooking: 2 hours	chutney

SERVES: 4

VARTA KOZI MASALA

This spicy fried chicken dish is a favorite from South India.

Ingredients

Chicken drumsticks	2 lb/12	Ginger paste	½ oz/3 tsp
Chick-pea flour	1 oz/2 tbs	Green chillies, chopped	3
Curry leaves	10	Oil to deep fry	
Flour	1 oz/2 tbs	Lemon juice	1 fl oz/2 tbs
Garlic paste	½ oz/3 tsp	Red chilli powder	¼ oz/1 tsp
Ginger, chopped	¼ oz/1 tsp	Salt to taste	

Method

1. Make a marinade of ginger and garlic pastes, red chilli powder, green chillies, ginger, curry leaves, salt and lemon juice.
2. Rub onto chicken and set aside for 2 hours.
3. Add flour and chick-pea flour to the marinade. Mix well.

4. Deep fry chicken, a few pieces at a time, in moderately hot oil. Remove and keep aside.
5. When all the pieces are done repeat the frying process to get a crisp exterior. The oil should not be too hot as it would then discolor the pieces.

Time	**To Serve**
Preparation: 2¼ hours	Serve with French fries, salad and mint
Cooking: 20 minutes	chutney

TANDOORI FISH

Whole fish, marinated and grilled.

Ingredients

Sole or plaice	4, each 1 lb	Lemon juice	1 fl oz/2 tbs
Carom (*ajwain*) seeds	¼ oz/1 tsp	Oil for brushing	
Cream	1½ fl oz/3 tbs	Red chilli powder	¼ oz/1 tsp
Cumin (*jeera*) powder	¼ oz/1 tsp	Salt to taste	
Garlic paste	¾ oz/4 tsp	Turmeric (*haldi*) powder	¼ oz/1 tsp
Ginger paste	¾ oz/4 tsp	White pepper powder	⅛ oz/½ tsp
Gram flour (*besan*)	¾ oz/4 tsp	Yoghurt	2 oz/¼ cup

Method

1. Clean fish and make 3-4 deep cuts on each side.

2. Hang yoghurt in a cheesecloth for 2 hours to remove whey.

3. Mix yoghurt with cream, ginger and garlic pastes, carom seeds, gram flour, white pepper, red chilli and cumin powders, lemon juice, salt and turmeric.

4. Rub mixture on both sides of the fish. Set aside for 2 hours.

5. Skewer fish from mouth to tail and roast in a hot tandoor or grill for 6 minutes or in a preheated oven at 350 °F for 10 minutes.

6. Remove from oven. Hang skewers for 5-7 minutes to let excess moisture drip off.

7. Baste with oil and roast again for 5 minutes.

Tips

Time
Preparation: 4½ hours
Cooking: 15 minutes

To Serve
Serve with mint chutney and onion rings

TANDOORI PRAWNS

Juicy prawns roasted in a tangy marinade.

Ingredients

Prawns	12 king size	Lemon juice	4 fl oz/½ cup
Carom (*ajwain*) seeds	¼ oz/1 tsp	Salt to taste	
Chick-pea flour	1½ oz/3 tbs	Turmeric (*haldi*) powder	⅛ oz/½ tsp
Chaat masala	¼ oz/1 tsp	White butter for basting	
Garam masala	¼ oz/1 tsp	Red chilli powder	¼ oz/1 tsp
Garlic paste	1½ oz/3 tbs	Yoghurt	17 oz/2 cups
Ginger paste	1½ oz/3 tbs		

Method

1. Reserve 2 tablespoons lemon juice and mix the rest with the ginger and garlic pastes.
2. Add salt, chick-pea flour, carom seeds, yoghurt, red chilli powder, garam masala and turmeric.
3. Marinade the prawns for 2 hours. Arrange on skewers and cook in a tandoor till half done, about 15 minutes.

4. Remove and set aside for 10 minutes. Cook again in the tandoor for 2 minutes.
5. Baste with butter and replace in the tandoor for approximately 3 more minutes.
6. Remove from skewers and arrange on a platter. Sprinkle with chaat masala and the reserved lemon juice.

Tips

Time
Preparation: 2 hours
Cooking: 15 minutes

To Serve
Serve with a green salad

SIKANDARI RAAN

An entire leg of lamb grilled with rum and spices.

Ingredients

Leg of lamb	3 lb/1 piece	Lemon juice	1 fl oz/2 tbs
Cardamom powder	1/8 oz/1/2 tsp	Mace (*javitri*) powder	1/8 oz/1/2 tsp
Chaat masala	1/4 oz/1 tsp	Malt vinegar	8 fl oz/1 cup
Cooking oil	2 fl oz/4 tbs	Red chilli powder	1/4 oz/1 tsp
Garlic paste	1/4 oz/1 tsp	Rum	4 fl oz/1/2 cup
Ginger paste	1/4 oz/1 tsp	Salt to taste	

Method

1. Prick leg all over with a fork.

2. Marinate the leg in a mixture of salt, red chilli powder, ginger and garlic pastes, mace and cardamom powders and lemon juice. Set aside for 2 hours.

3. Pour the vinegar and rum over the lamb.

4. Place leg on a baking tray and pour over 32 fl oz/4 cups water. Bake in an oven at 350 °F for 1½ hours turning the leg two or three times to ensure it cooks evenly.

5. Once water dries out remove from tray. Baste with oil and grill till well done all over.

Time
Preparation: 2½ hours
Cooking: 2½ hours

To Serve
Garnish with onion rings and sliced tomato. Sprinkle chaat masala and serve hot

PATHAR KEBAB

Tangy lamb slices, marinated and cooked on a griddle in very little fat.

Ingredients

Lamb chops, deboned	½ lb	Onion paste, browned	1½ oz/3 tbs
Garam masala	a pinch	Raw papaya paste	½ oz/1 tbs
Ginger-garlic paste	1 oz/2 tbs	Red chilli powder	¼ oz/1 tsp
Lemon juice	½ fl oz/1 tbs	Salt to taste	
Malt vinegar	¼ fl oz/2 tsp	White pepper	⅛ oz/½ tsp
Mint, chopped	½ oz/1 tbs	Yoghurt	4 oz/½ cup
Oil	a few drops		

Method

1. Beat the lamb slices till tender. Apply malt vinegar, salt, ginger-garlic paste, white pepper, raw papaya paste, lemon juice, red chilli powder, chopped mint, yoghurt and garam masala.

2. Marinate for 2 hours.
3. Grease a griddle.
4. Place the slices on the griddle and cook both sides on a slow flame evenly till well browned.

Time
Preparation: 2 hours
Cooking: 20 minutes

To Serve
Serve on a platter with fresh salad

KAKORI KEBAB

*These delicate, melt-in-the-mouth, mince kebabs, are usually made
on festive occasions.*

Ingredients

Ground lamb	2.2 lb	Oil for basting	
Black pepper	¼ oz/1 tsp	Onion, chopped	6 oz/¾ cup
Butter for basting		Onion paste, browned	2 oz/¼ cup
Cashew nuts	2 oz/¼ cup	Poppy seeds (*khus khus*)	2 oz/¼ cup
Cloves	⅛ oz/½ tsp	Raw papaya	2 oz/¼ cup
Cooking oil	8 fl oz/1 cup	Red chilli powder	¼ oz/1 tsp
Garam masala	¼ oz/1 tsp	Saffron	⅛ oz/1 tsp
Gram flour (*besan*), roasted	3½ oz/7 tbs	Vetiver (*kewda*) essence	2 drops
Green cardamom powder	¼ oz/1 tsp		

Method

1. Grind lamb twice and a third time with the oil.

2. Blend all the other ingredients (except saffron, red chilli powder and vetiver) together and mix with the mince.

3. Add red chilli powder, saffron and vetiver. Knead well.

4. Set aside for half an hour. Knead again.

5. Pat the mixture in a thin layer around the skewers and cook over low charcoal fire for 5 minutes.

6. Baste with butter and cook again for 4 minutes.

7. Transfer to an oven at 325 °F for 8 minutes. Baste with butter and roast again for 4 minutes.

Tips

Time
Preparation: 1 hour
Cooking: 20 minutes

To Serve
Serve hot with sheermal. For recipe see
p. 62

SHAMI KEBAB

Delicate and crumbly, these kebabs are a spicer variation of the minced meat cutlets.

Ingredients

Ground meat	2 lb		Garlic cloves, chopped	6
Bengal gram (*kaala chana*), split and husked	1½ oz/3 tbs		Ginger, chopped	½ oz/1 tbs
Black peppercorns	6		Green chillies, chopped	4
Cardamoms	4		Mint, dry leaves powdered	⅛ oz/½ tsp
Cinnamon	1" piece		Oil for frying	
Coriander leaves, chopped	½ oz/1 tbs		Onions, chopped	5 oz/⅔ cup
Coriander powder	¼ oz/1 tsp		Poppy seeds, well pounded	¾ oz/⅓ tsp
Cream	½ fl oz/1 tbs		Red chillies	5
Cumin (*jeera*) seeds	¼ oz/1 tsp		Salt to taste	

Method

1. Cook ground meat, gram, cumin seeds, cardamoms, garlic, ginger, cinnamon, red chillies, poppy seeds, peppercorns, coriander powder and half the onions in 16 fl oz/ 2 cups of water for 40 minutes or till meat is cooked and all liquid has evaporated. **2.** Remove fibres from meat if any. Grind in a food processor till a thick paste is obtained. **3.** Add the left over onions, coriander leaves, mint leaves, green chillies and cream. **4.** Mix thoroughly. Make small 2 inch cakes and cook on a griddle or frying pan with very little oil. When one side is browned (3 minutes) turn over and fry the other

Time	**To Serve**
Preparation: 45 minutes Cooking: 1 hour	Garnish with onion rings and serve hot

SERVES: 4

TALA GOSHT

A quick, delicious dish of fried lamb if meat has been marinated in advance.

Ingredients

Boneless lamb	1½ lb	Ginger, grated	½ oz/3 tsp
Black peppercorns	⅛ oz/½ tsp	Green chillies, chopped fine	4
Cooking oil	1 fl oz/2 tbs	Red chilli powder	⅛ oz/½ tsp
Garam masala	⅛ oz/½ tsp	Salt to taste	
Garlic paste	¼ oz/1 tsp		

Method

1. Chop meat into tiny pieces, a quarter inch thick. Pound the pieces till they flatten slightly.

2. Mix ginger, garlic, green chillies, red chilli powder and salt.

3. Rub mixture onto meat. Grind peppercorns and rub onto meat. Set aside for 2 hours.

4. Heat oil in a pan over medium flame. Put in the meat. Let simmer for 5 minutes. Stir occasionally. Cover and cook till the meat is tender.

5. Remove cover and turn up heat. Add garam masala.

6. Cook till all moisture has evaporated and meat is browned.

Time	**To Serve**
Preparation: 2½ hours Cooking: 15 minutes	Serve on toothpicks with mint sprigs and lime wedges as a cocktail snack, or with a daal and any flaky bread

PESHAWARI KEBAB

Succulent lamb pieces coated with raw papaya and yoghurt and roasted till crisp on the outside.

Ingredients

Boneless lamb	2.2 lb	Ginger paste	½ oz/1 tbs
Black cumin		Juice of 1 lemon	
(*shah jeera*) seeds	¼ oz/1 tsp	Raw papaya paste	¼ oz/1 tsp
Chaat masala	¼ oz/1 tsp	Red chilli powder	¼ oz/1 tsp
Clarified butter for basting		Salt to taste	
Garam masala	¼ oz/1 tsp	Yoghurt	4 oz/½ cup
Garlic paste	¼ oz/1 tsp		

Method

1. Cut meat into 1 inch cubes. Marinate with salt, red chilli powder, garam masala, papaya paste, black cumin, ginger and garlic pastes and yoghurt. Mix well and leave aside for an hour.

2. Put meat pieces on skewers and cook in a tandoor till half done.
3. Leave to cool for 10 minutes.
4. Baste with clarified butter and cook for 8 more minutes.

Time
Preparation: 1¼ hours
Cooking: 30 minutes

To Serve
Sprinkle with chaat masala and lemon juice. Serve with a green salad

PAKE GOSHT KE KEBAB

These lamb kebabs are made with partially cooked meat, so that the flavor of the spices works right in.

Ingredients

Lean lamb, shoulder cuts	2.2 lb	Onions, chopped	8¾ oz/1 cup
Cooking oil	1 fl oz/2 tbs	Red chilli powder	⅛ oz/½ tsp
Coriander powder	1 oz/2 tbs	Salt to taste	
Garam masala	⅛ oz/½ tsp	Turmeric	⅛ oz/½ tsp
Ginger, grated	¼ oz/1 tsp	Yoghurt	8¾ oz/1 cup
Lemon juice	1 fl oz/2 tbs		

Method

1. Beat to a creamy smoothness half the yoghurt with coriander powder, ginger, chilli powder, lemon juice, oil and salt.

2. Add onions and meat cut into 2 inch cubes. Leave to marinate for an hour.

3. To the other half of the yoghurt add turmeric and garam masala and whip. Add the meat mixture and transfer to a pan.

4. Put pan on stove and heat slowly till mixture begins to simmer. Cover and cook on low heat for 40 minutes till meat is almost done.

5. Remove lid and let all moisture evaporate till only a thick sauce-like coating remains on the meat pieces.

6. Skewer meat pieces and roast in a medium hot tandoor or grill lightly on a tray, turning regularly till all sides are evenly browned.

Tips

Time
Preparation: 1½ hours
Cooking: 1 hour

To Serve
Remove from skewers and serve hot with any Indian bread or rice

SEEKH KEBAB

Spicy minced meat rolled on to skewers and roasted. Aromatic and velvety smooth.

Ingredients

Ground meat	1 lb	Ginger paste	½ oz/3 tsp
Black cardamoms	2	Gram flour (*besan*), roasted	1½ oz/3 tbs
Black peppercorns	¼ oz/1 tsp	Mace (*javitri*) powder	⅛ oz/½ tsp
Cinnamon powder	⅛ oz/½ tsp	Oil	½ fl oz/1 tbs
Cloves	2	Onion paste, browned	1½ oz/3 tbs
Coconut, grated	½ oz/1 tbs	Poppy seeds (*khus khus*)	¼ oz/1 tsp
Cream	1 fl oz/2 tbs	Raw papaya paste	½ oz/1 tbs
Cumin (*jeera*) seeds	¼ oz/1 tsp	Red chilli powder	¼ oz/1 tsp
Garlic paste	½ oz/3 tsp	Yoghurt	1 oz/2 tbs

Method

1. Mix mince with all other ingredients.
2. Knead well for 10 minutes.
3. Let stand for 10 minutes.
4. Moisten hands with cold water and mould mixture around skewers pressing and shaping to the size of a frankfurter sausage, about 5½ inches long.

5. Roast the kebabs in a moderately hot tandoor for 12 minutes till they are browned uniformly. The kebabs can also be slid off the skewers and cooked on the fine wire mesh of the grilling rack in a charcoal gas grill. Do not turn too often as the kebabs may split.

Tips

Time
Preparation: 45 minutes
Cooking: 15 minutes

To Serve
Serve hot with mint chutney

BARAH KEBAB

SERVES: 4

Literally the 'big' kebab. Huge lamb chops, skewered and roasted for a hearty meal.

Ingredients

Lamb chops & leg pieces	2 lb	Malt vinegar	6 fl oz/¾ cup
Black cumin		Oil for basting	
(*shab jeera*) seeds	1½ oz/3 tbs	Raw papaya paste	¾ oz/4 tsp
Garam masala	¾ oz/4 tsp	Red chilli powder	½ oz/1 tbs
Garlic paste	1½ oz/3 tbs	Salt to taste	
Ginger paste	1½ oz/3 tbs	Yoghurt	2 oz/¼ cup
Kachri (tenderizer)	¾ oz/4 tsp		

Method

1. Marinate the lamb in salt, red chilli powder, garam masala, malt vinegar, ginger and garlic pastes, papaya paste, kachri and cumin seeds for 4 hours or overnight.

2. Skewer pieces 1 inch apart and roast on a slow fire in a tandoor or charcoal grill for 15 minutes or till half done.

3. Stand at room temperature for 20 minutes. Baste with oil.

4. Roast or grill on slow fire for another 20 minutes, till velvety brown.

SERVES: 4

SHIKAMPURI KEBAB

Spicy minced lamb kebabs with a soft centre filling of yoghurt, mint and onions.

Ingredients

Lamb, ground	2 lb	Mace (*javitri*) powder	¼ oz/1 tsp
Bengal gram		Mint, chopped	½ oz/1 tbs
(*kaala chana*), split	8¾ oz/1 cup	Oil for deep frying	
Coriander leaves, chopped	¾ oz/4 tsp	Onions, chopped fine	5 oz/²⁄₃ cup
Egg whites	2	Onion paste, browned	1½ oz/3 tbs
Flour	1 oz/6 tsp	Red chilli powder	¼ oz/1 tsp
Garam masala	¾ oz/4 tsp	Salt to taste	
Green chillies, chopped	1½ oz/3 tbs	Yoghurt, hung	2 oz/¼ cup

Method

1. Mix together yoghurt, mint and half cup chopped onions and keep aside.
2. Boil the ground meat and Bengal gram in a little water till cooked and dry. Grind into a paste without using any water.
3. Mix together salt, browned onion paste, left over chopped onions, green chillies, coriander, garam masala, mace, red chilli powder, egg whites and flour and add to the mince.
4. Mix well and roll into tight balls to fit the palm of your hand.
5. Make a deep groove in the ball with the thumb. Stuff with a large pinch of the yoghurt, onion and mint mixture and seal.
6. Roll between palms to smoothen surface.
7. Flatten slightly into patty shapes and deep fry.

KALEJI KEBAB

Liver, fried and cooked on skewers.

Ingredients

Liver	½ lb	Ginger paste	¼ oz/1 tsp
Black cardamoms	2	Oil	2 fl oz/¼ cup
Cinnamon	1	Onions, grated	2 oz/¼ cup
Coriander leaves, chopped	¾ oz/4 tsp	Onion paste	1 oz/2 tbs
Coriander seeds, roasted	¼ oz/1 tsp	Red chilli powder	⅛ oz/½ tsp
Cumin (*jeera*) seeds	⅛ oz/½ tsp	Salad oil	2 fl oz/¼ cup
Garam masala	⅛ oz/½ tsp	Salt to taste	
Garlic cloves, chopped	4	Tomatoes, chopped	4 oz/½ cup
Garlic paste	¼ oz/1 tsp	Turmeric (*haldi*) powder	¼ oz/1 tsp
Ginger, shredded	¼ oz/1" piece	Yoghurt	2 oz/¼ cup

Method

1. Cut liver into 1 inch cubes.

2. Beat together yoghurt and salad oil. Mix in ginger, garlic and onion pastes, salt and turmeric. Add the liver pieces and leave for an hour.

3. Blend together roasted coriander seeds, cumin seeds, cloves, cinnamon, cardamoms, chopped ginger and garlic in a mixer with a little water.

4. Remove liver cubes from the marinade. Heat the cooking oil in a flat pan and sauté liver cubes gently. Remove.

5. In the same oil add grated onion and sauté till golden brown.

6. Add red chilli powder to the oil with a tablespoon of warm water and stir.

7. Add the ginger, garlic and blended paste and the left over marinade.

8. Stir-cook for 5 minutes. Put liver on skewers and place on pan.

9. Cover and cook for 5 minutes.

10. Finally, add chopped tomatoes. Cook for another 5 minutes, turning skewers around a couple of times. Cook till tomatoes are done. Remove from heat.

Tips

Time
Preparation: 1 hour
Cooking: 30 minutes

To Serve
Transfer to a flat dish with the skewers, sprinkle with garam masala and green coriander leaves. Serve hot with any Indian bread

KATHI KEBAB

*The most elementary of kebabs, rolled in a roti or paratha
to make a complete meal.*

Ingredients

Lean lamb	1 lb in 1" cubes	Dry mango powder (*amchur*)	¼ oz/1 tsp
Black cardamoms	4	Onions, chopped	2.5 oz/⅓ cup
Black peppercorns	15	Poppy seeds (*khus khus*)	⅛ oz/½ tsp
Butter for brushing		Red chilli powder	¼ oz/1 tsp
Cinnamon	1" piece	Roasted gram, powdered	½ oz/1 tbs
Cloves	6	Rotis or parathas	4
Coriander seeds	¼ oz/1 tsp	Salad oil	½ oz/1 tbs
Cumin (*jeera*) seeds	¼ oz/1 tsp	Salt to taste	
Garam masala	¼ oz/1 tsp	Tenderizer	¼ oz/1 tsp
Garlic, chopped	10 cloves	Turmeric	¼ oz/1 tsp
Ginger, chopped	½ oz/2" piece	Yoghurt	4 oz/½ cup
Lemon juice	½ fl oz/1 tbs		

Method

1. Beat lamb cubes with mallet to flatten them slightly.

2. Lightly broil poppy and coriander seeds, cloves, cardamoms, cinnamon, peppercorns and cumin. Blend these in a mixer along with the onion, garlic and ginger. Mix in yoghurt, salt, red chilli powder, turmeric, tenderizer, gram flour and oil.

3. Coat lamb cubes with the mixture then string them on skewers.

4. Roast over an open charcoal fire or a hot grill at 325 °F for 12-15 minutes, turning 2-3 times.

5. When done, brush with butter. Sprinkle mango powder, garam masala and lemon juice on kebabs. Divide into four, placing each portion on one roti or paratha. Roll tighly wrapping one end in aluminium foil or butter paper.

Note: Lamb can be substituted with chicken or paneer cubes.

Time	To Serve
Preparation: 30 minutes	Serve with mint chutney and onion salad
Cooking: 15 minutes	

SERVES: 4

GALOUTI KEBAB

A velvet smooth, cardamom flavored minced lamb kebab.

Ingredients

Lamb, ground	3.3 oz	Oil to shallow fry			
Cardamom powder	¼ oz/1 tsp	Raw papaya paste	2½ oz/5 tbs		
Garlic paste	1½ oz/3 tbs	Red chilli powder	¼ oz/1 tsp		
Ginger paste	1½ oz/3 tbs	Roasted gram, powdered	1½ oz/3 tbs		
Mace (*javitri*) powder	⅛ oz/½ tsp	Salt to taste			

Method

1. Freeze ground meat for 15 minutes.

2. Mix the ginger, garlic and papaya pastes, red chilli powder, salt, mace, cardamom and roasted gram flour with the ground meat.

3. Divide into 28 portions and roll into balls between the palms.

4. Flatten balls slightly and shallow fry over low heat till both sides are light brown.

Time
Preparation: 1 hour
Cooking: 20 minutes

To Serve
Serve with mint chutney and biryani. For recipe see p. 61 of the *Curries & Simmering Pot* section

SERVES: 4

PASINDA KEBAB

Thin meat slices roasted on skewers.

Ingredients

A slab of lean meat	1 lb	Kachri (tenderizer) or	¼ oz/1 tsp
Butter for basting		Raw papaya paste	¼ oz/1 tsp
Black peppercorns	16	Red chilli powder	¼ oz/1 tsp
Cardamoms	5	Nutmeg (*jaiphal*) powder	a pinch
Cloves	5	Onions, chopped	2 oz/¼ cup
Coconut, desiccated	1 oz/2 tbs	Poppy seeds (*khus khus*)	¼ oz/1 tsp
Cumin (*jeera*) seeds	¼ oz/1 tsp	Salt to taste	
Garlic, chopped	10 cloves	Yoghurt	5 oz/⅔ cup
Ginger, chopped	½ oz/2" piece		

Method

1. Cut meat into slices 3½ inches long, 1¼ inches wide and three-fourths of an inch thick. Cut the slice into half without cutting through, leaving a join at the end. Open the cut halves to make a single strip, approximately 6 inches long. Beat the joints with the back of a knife to flatten them a bit.
2. In a mixer blend together cloves, cardamoms, papaya or kachri, garlic, onion, ginger, cumin, coconut, nutmeg, peppercorns, poppy seeds and yoghurt. Add red chilli powder and salt.
3. Coat the strips with this mixture and leave to marinate for 3 hours.
4. Weave the skewer in and out of the meat strips at 4 points, at regular intervals. The meat will resemble a wavy line, with the skewer running through its centre.
5. Roast over an open charcoal fire or barbeque for 10 minutes. When one side is cooked, baste with butter and roast again for 3-5 minutes.

Time
Preparation: 3½ hours
Cooking: 15 minutes

To Serve
Serve as a salad with sliced onions, green chillies and finely cut mint leaves

39

TANDOORI CAPSICUM

These stuffed and grilled peppers are delightfully different.

Ingredients

Capsicum,		thinly sliced	2 oz/¼ cup
medium sized	½ lb/4 pieces	Garam masala	a pinch
Cabbage, shredded	4 oz/½ cup	Garlic paste	⅛ oz/½ tsp
Cashew nuts, broken	¼ oz/1 tsp	Ginger paste	⅛ oz/½ tsp
Coriander leaves, chopped	¼ oz/1 tsp	Green peas	¾ oz/4 tsp
Carrots, grated	2.5 oz/⅓ cup	Oil	½ fl oz/1 tbs
Cottage cheese, grated	8¾ oz/1 cup	Raisins	¼ oz/1 tsp
Cumin (*jeera*) seeds	⅛ oz/½ tsp	Red chilli powder	⅛ oz/½ tsp
French beans,		Salt to taste	

Method

1. Cut the capsicums at the stem end and scoop out the seeds.

2. Heat oil. Add cumin and splutter. Add ginger and garlic pastes and fry for a few minutes.

3. Add all vegetables and stir-fry. Add salt and red chilli powder.

4. Fry till the oil surfaces. Take off fire.

5. Add grated cottage cheese and garam masala.

6. Cool mixture. Add cashew nuts, raisins and coriander.

7. Stuff the capsicums with the mixture and put a skewer through them. Grill for 5 minutes or bake in a tandoor for 8 minutes.

Tips

Time
Preparation: 15-20 minutes
Cooking: 15 minutes

To Serve
Put on a platter and decorate with lemon wedges, onion rings and tomato rings

TANDOORI PHOOL

Batter fried cauliflower, roasted to a perfect crispness in the tandoor.

Ingredients

Cauliflowers	1¾ lb/2 small flowers	Lemon	2
Chaat masala	¾ oz/4 tsp	Oil to fry	
Cooking oil	1 fl oz/2 tbs	Red chilli powder	¼ oz/1 tsp
Cucumber, sliced	1	Salt to taste	
Gram flour (*besan*)	2 oz/4 tbs	Tomato wedges	8

Method

1. Break the cauliflower into florets, wash thoroughly then dry.

2. Marinate the florets in a mixture of salt, chaat masala and lemon juice for 30 minutes.

3. Make a smooth batter of the gram flour with 4 fl oz/½ cup water. Season with salt and red chilli powder.

4. Heat oil in a frying pan. Dip the florets into the batter and fry in the hot oil over a low flame.

5. Remove. Once the florets are cool, cut into pieces.

6. Put on skewers and roast in a tandoor for 5-6 minutes till golden brown or roast in a preheated oven at 275 °F for 10 minutes. Baste with oil while roasting.

Time
Preparation: 45 minutes
Cooking: 20 minutes

To Serve
Remove from skewers and serve with sliced cucumber and tomato wedges

SERVES: 4

HARA KEBAB

Cottage cheese and spinach blended together to give an unusual green color.

Ingredients

Cottage cheese, grated		1 lb
Spinach, boiled and blended		2 lb
Cardamom powder	¼ oz/1 tsp	
Cashew nuts	4 oz/½ cup	
Coriander leaves, chopped	¾ oz/4 tsp	
Garam masala	¾ oz/4 tsp	
Ginger paste	1½ oz/3 tbs	
Gram flour (besan), roasted	2 oz/¼ cup	
Green chillies, chopped	15	
Mace (javitri) powder	¼ oz/1 tsp	
Oil for deep frying		
Salt to taste		

Method

1. Mix together all ingredients except oil and shape into 1½ inch round patties.

2. Heat oil in a frying pan and deep fry.

Time

Preparation: 30 minutes
Cooking: 15 minutes

To Serve

Garnish with onion rings and serve as a snack or as an accompaniment with a rice and curry dish

DAHI KE KEBAB

These unusual, succulent kebabs have yoghurt as the main ingredient.

Ingredients

Yoghurt, thick	1 lb	Garlic paste	¼ oz/1 tsp
Black pepper powder	⅛ oz/½ tsp	Milk	2 fl oz/¼ cup
Cardamom powder	⅛ oz/½ tsp	Onions, sliced fine	2 oz/¼ cup
Cinnamon powder	a large pinch	Red chilli powder	¼ oz/1 tsp
Cloves powder	¼ oz/1 tsp	Roasted gram, powdered	4 oz/½ cup
Cooking oil	4 fl oz/½ cup	Salt to taste	

Method

1. Hang yoghurt in a muslin cloth for 2 hours till all the whey drains out.

2. Add roasted gram, salt and half of all the spices (red chilli, clove, cardamom, cinnamon and black pepper powders) to the curd and mix well.

3. Divide into 20 equal parts. Flatten to get a smooth, even shape.

4. Heat oil in a pan and fry kebabs, a few at a time, to a light golden color. Keep aside.

5. In the same oil, fry onions till crisp and golden brown. Remove. Cool and grind the onions.

6. Now add salt, garlic paste, ground onions and remaining half of all the spices to the oil. Stir-cook for a few minutes.

7. Add kebabs. Turn gently till each piece is coated with the masala. Sprinkle milk on the kebabs. Let sizzle for 10 seconds.

Tips

Time
Preparation: 2½ hours
Cooking: 30 minutes

To Serve
Serve at once as part of the main course

GOOLAR KEBAB

A vegetarian delicacy, this wild fig kebab is very much like meat in flavor and texture.

Ingredients

Wild figs (*goolar*)	½ lb	Oil to shallow fry	
Bengal gram (*kaala chana*),		Onions, chopped fine	2 oz/¼ cup
split and husked	2 oz/¼ cup	Red chilli powder	¼ oz/1 tsp
Cumin (*jeera*) seeds	½ oz/1 tsp	Salt to taste	
Garam masala	⅛ oz/½ tsp	Turmeric (*haldi*) powder	⅛ oz/½ tsp
Garlic paste	¼ oz/1 tsp	Vinegar	a few drops

Method

1. Wash and quarter each fig. Soak in water for 2 hours. Stir occasionally. Drain off any dirt which floats to the surface of the water.
2. Soak chopped onions in the vinegar. Keep aside
3. In a pan put to boil fig pieces, gram, salt, red chilli powder, cumin seeds, turmeric and garlic paste with 2 fl oz/¼ cup water.
4. Cover and cook till the gram and figs are tender. Dry out moisture completely.

5. Add garam masala and grind the fig, gram and spice mixture to a fine paste.
6. Divide into 12 equal portions. Flatten each portion between the palms.
7. Stuff with a large pinch of chopped onions and roll into a smooth, even ball.
8. Flatten slightly with wet hands and shallow fry on low heat, till both sides are dark brown.

Time
Preparation: 2 hours
Cooking: 2 hours

To Serve
Can be served as a starter with mint chutney or as part of the main course

PANEER TIKKA

An exotic, easy to cook cottage cheese kebab for vegetarians.

Ingredients

Cottage cheese	1¾ lb	Garam masala	¼ oz/1 tsp
Carom (*ajwain*) seeds	¼ oz/1 tsp	Gram flour (*besan*)	1 oz/2 tbs
Cream	¾ fl oz/4 tsp	Salt to taste	
Cumin (*jeera*) seeds	¼ oz/1 tsp	Turmeric (*haldi*) powder	⅛ oz/½ tsp
Egg	1	White pepper powder	⅛ oz/½ tsp

Method

1. Cut cottage cheese into 2 inch cubes.

2. Sprinkle cumin, carom, white pepper, turmeric, salt and half the garam masala on the cheese and set aside for 15 minutes.

3. Whip egg in a bowl. Add gram flour, cream and salt. Coat cottage cheese pieces with the mixture and set aside for 45 minutes.

4. Skewer the cottage cheese pieces 1 inch apart. Skewer a peeled whole onion at the end to prevent the tikkas slipping out.

5. Roast in a moderately hot oven or charcoal grill for 12 minutes or in a preheated oven for 14 minutes.

Time
Preparation: 1½ hours
Cooking: 15 minutes

To Serve
Serve as a vegetarian snack or with rice and daal bukhara. For recipe see p. 17 of the **Vegetarian Dishes & Desserts** section

SERVES: 4

NADRU SHAMI KEBAB

An exotic vegetarian snack made from lotus stems.

Ingredients

Lotus stem	2 lb	Green chillies, chopped	2 oz/¼ cup	
Bengal gram		Oil to fry		
(*kaala chana*), split and husked	9 oz	Onions, chopped	2.5 oz/⅓ cup	
Chaat masala	¼ oz/1 tsp	Red chilli powder	¼ oz/1 tsp	
Coriander leaves, chopped	¾ oz/4 tsp	Roasted gram, powdered	1½ oz/3 tbs	
Garam masala	¾ oz/4 tsp	Salt to taste		

Method

1. Thoroughly wash and chop lotus stem. Put to boil in a pan with some water together with the Bengal gram. Cook till tender and dry.
2. Grind the two to a thick paste without using any water.
3. Add all other ingredients except oil to the paste. Knead for 5 minutes.
4. Shape into small cutlets and deep fry in hot oil.

Time
Preparation: 45 minutes
Cooking: 1 hour

To Serve
Serve hot as a snack with mint chutney

SERVES: 4

HARE CHANE KA KEBAB

Fresh, green gram patties make a tasty and filling snack.

Ingredients

Fresh Bengal gram (*hara chana*), shelled	17 oz/2 cups	Green chilli paste	1½ oz/3 tbs
		Oil to deep fry	
Cooking oil	1 fl oz/2 tbs	Onion paste	2 oz/4 tbs
Coriander powder	¼ oz/1 tsp	Roasted gram, powdered	1 oz/6 tsp
Cumin (*jeera*) powder	⅛ oz/½ tsp	Salt to taste	
Garam masala	a large pinch	Sugar, powdered	⅛ oz/½ tsp
Garlic paste	1 oz/6 tsp	Yoghurt	4 oz/½ cup

Method

1. Boil the Bengal gram along with the salt, coriander powder, cumin powder, green chilli, onion and garlic pastes, yoghurt and 1 fl oz/2 tablespoons oil in 16 fl oz/2 cups of water.

2. Cook till gram is tender and all moisture has evaporated.

3. Grind to a thick paste without using any water. Add the roasted gram, garam masala and sugar and knead well till a smooth and soft dough is formed.

4. Divide the dough into 12 equal parts. Flatten each portion into round patty shapes.

5. Heat oil and deep fry on low heat.

Tips

Time
Preparation: 30 minutes
Cooking: 1 hour

To Serve
Serve hot with mint chutney as a snack

TANDOORI ALOO

Potatoes stuffed with lightly spiced cottage cheese and grilled in a tandoor.

Ingredients

Large potatoes	2.2 lb/8	Garam masala	a pinch
Cashew nuts, broken	5-10/1 tbs	Lemon juice	¼ fl oz/2 tsp
Chaat masala	⅛ oz/½ tsp	Oil for frying	
Clarified butter (*ghee*)	¼ oz/1 tsp	Red chilli powder	¼ oz/1 tsp
Coriander leaves, chopped	¼ oz/1 tsp	Raisins	¼ oz/1 tsp
Cottage cheese, grated	¾ oz/4 tsp	Salt to taste	
Cumin seeds (*jeera*)	⅛ oz/½ tsp		

Method

1. Peel the potatoes. Scoop out the center leaving thin walls at the sides.

2. Fry the potato shells and the scoops seperately. Do not let them change color but let the sides become crisp.

3. Cool the scooped out portion of the potatoes and mash. Add salt, red chilli powder, garam masala, lemon juice, cashew nuts, raisins and clarified butter.

4. Stuff the mixture into the potato cases.

5. Arrange 4 pieces on one skewer and put grated cheese on top. Grill till golden brown in color.

Tips

Time
Preparation: 20 minutes
Cooking: 15 minutes

To Serve
Sprinkle with chopped coriander and chaat masala and serve

TANDOORI SALAD

A light, healthy salad, grilled to give it a smooth texture.

Ingredients

Capsicum, deseeded and sliced	¼ lb	Onions, sliced	5 oz/⅔ cup
Chaat masala	¾ oz/4 tsp	Pineapple slices, drained	17 oz/2 cups
Cottage cheese, cubed	5 oz/⅔ cup	Salad oil	8 fl oz/1 cup
Garam masala	¾ oz/4 tsp	Salt to taste	
Lemon juice	½ fl oz/1 tbs	Tomatoes,	
Lemon wedges	24	halved	½ lb/14-16 pieces

Method

1. Cut cottage cheese and pineapple slices into 1 inch cubes.

2. Add chaat masala, garam masala, lemon juice, salt and salad oil to the capsicum

onions and tomatoes. Toss well together.

3. Skewer the vegetables, cottage cheese and pineapple cubes in turn.

4. Cook on a slow grill for 10 minutes.

Time	To Serve
Preparation: 30 minutes	Remove from skewer onto a platter and
Cooking: 15 minutes	serve with the lemon wedges

SERVES: 4

SHALGAM KE KEBAB

Turnips boiled and ground to make delicious patties which melt in the mouth.

Ingredients

Turnips, quartered	2½-2¼ lb	Red chilli powder	⅛ oz/½ tsp
Garam masala	a large pinch	Roasted gram, powdered	1 oz/2 tbs
Oil to shallow fry		Salt to taste	
Onions, sliced fine	2 oz/¼ cup		

Method

1. Fry sliced onions in 1 tablespoon oil till golden brown and crisp. Grind coarsely.

2. Boil turnips in water. When cooked discard the water.

3. Taking a few pieces of turnip at a time, wrap them in muslin and squeeze out as much liquid as possible. Discard the liquid.

4. Mash turnips finely. Add salt, red chillies, garam masala, gram powder and ground onions. Mix and knead well.

5. Divide mixture into 8 equal parts.

6. Flatten and shape into patty rounds with wet palms.

7. Shallow fry on a griddle till golden brown.

Time	To Serve
Preparation: 30 minutes	Refry for a minute and serve hot with
Cooking; 1½ hours	biryani or pulao.

DUM SAUNFIA TIKKA

Cubes of cottage cheese, layered with fennel, mint and raisin chutney and grilled in the oven.

Ingredients

Cottage cheese	2 lb	Red chilli powder	¼ oz/1 tsp
Carom (*ajwain*) seeds	¼ oz/1 tsp	Salt to taste	
Cream	2 fl oz/¼ cup	Sugar	¼ oz/1 tsp
Fennel (*saunf*) seeds,		White pepper powder	¼ oz/1 tsp
powdered	¼ oz/1 tsp	Yoghurt	4 oz/½ cup
Mint chutney*	4 fl oz/½ cup		
Raisins	1 oz/2 tbs		

* For recipe see pp. 60-61 of the ***Vegetarian Dishes & Desserts*** section

Method

1. Hang yoghurt in a cheese cloth for 2 hours, till whey is drained.

2. Add cream to the yoghurt and mix in red chilli powder, white pepper powder, carom and salt.

3. Add raisins, fennel powder and sugar to the mint chutney.

4. Cut cottage cheese into 1½ inch cubes. Slit the cubes and spread with mint chutney.

5. Press halves together again.

6. Marinate the cheese cubes in the yoghurt-cream-spice mixture for 15 minutes.

7. Put on skewers and cook in a preheated oven at 275 °F for 5 minutes.

Tips

Time
Preparation: 30 minutes
Cooking: 10 minutes

To Serve
Serve hot as a vegetarian cocktail snack

KHAMEERI ROTI

SERVES: 4

Leavened bread.

Ingredients

Wholewheat flour	17 oz/2 cups	
Clarified butter (*ghee*) to grease baking tray.		
Flour to dust		
Yeast, fresh		Salt to taste
		¼ oz/1 tsp

Method

1. Dissolve the yeast in 4 fl oz/half cup warm water.

2. Sift the flour with salt onto a platter.

3. Make a well in the flour and pour 8 fl oz/1 cup water. Mix flour and water gradually, then knead into a tough dough. Cover with a damp cloth and keep aside for 15 minutes.

4. Slowly sprinkle the dissolved yeast over the dough and keep kneading till the dough is smooth and pliable and not sticky. Cover with damp cloth and set aside for 30 minutes.

5. Divide dough into 8 equal balls and dust with dry flour.

6. Press and flatten each ball into round discs, 8 inches wide. Wearing an oven glove stick the disc to the side of a hot tandoor and bake for 2 minutes. Remove with a pair of tongs. Alternatively, place on a greased baking tray and bake for 4-5 minutes in a preheated oven at 350 °F.

Tip

Time
Preparation: 1 hour
Cooking: 4-5 minutes for each roti

To Serve
Serve hot with curry

TAFTAN

A rich, leavened, rice flour bread.

Ingredients

Rice flour	17 oz/2 cups	Milk	8 fl oz/1 cup
Butter or clarified		Salt to taste	
butter (*ghee*) for brushing		Sugar	$^{1}/_{8}$ oz/$^{1}/_{2}$ tsp
Clarified butter (*ghee*)	6 oz/$^{3}/_{4}$ cup	Water	4 fl oz/$^{1}/_{2}$ cup
Coriander leaves, chopped	$^{1}/_{4}$ oz/1 tsp	Yeast	$^{1}/_{8}$ oz/$^{1}/_{2}$ tsp
Melon (*magaz*) seeds	$^{1}/_{4}$ oz/1 tsp		

Method

1. Sift flour and salt together.
2. Make a well in the flour and add water, sugar, milk, ghee, yeast and melon seeds. Mix gradually and knead into a soft dough.
3. Divide into 4 equal balls and set aside for half an hour.
4. Dust lightly and roll into 3½ inch discs, a quarter of an inch thick. Sprinkle with coriander.
5. Put into tandoor and bake till brown in color.
6. Brush with ghee.

Tips

Time
Preparation: 1 hour
Cooking: 10 minutes for each taftan

To serve
Serve hot with any curry.

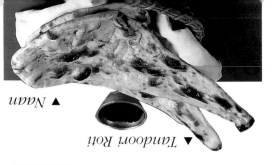

▲ *Naan*

▲ *Tandoori Roti*

▼ *Lachha Paratha*

▲ *Sheermal*

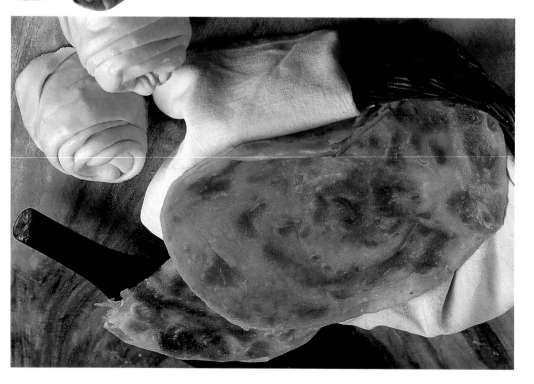

LACHHA PARATHA

A multi-layered bread, flavored with fennel.

Ingredients

Flour	17 oz/2 cups	Flour to dust	
Fennel (*saunf*)	¼ oz/1 tsp	Milk	8 fl oz/1 cup
Clarified butter (*ghee*)	6 oz/¾ cup	Salt to taste	
Clarified butter to shallow fry			

Method

1. Sift flour and salt together.

2. Pound fennel with a pestle.

3. Make a well in the flour and pour in milk and 4 fl oz/½ cup water. Mix gradually and knead into a dough. Cover with moist cloth and keep aside for 10 minutes.

4. Melt a third of the clarified butter (ghee) and add gradually to the dough, kneading constantly till a soft and smooth dough is obtained.

5. Add pounded fennel and knead for 5 minutes.

6. Divide and roll into 12 equal balls.

7. Dust lightly and roll into 6 inch discs, Apply ¼ oz/1 teaspoon ghee evenly over one side.

8. Make a radial cut and fold disc into a narrow conical shape. Place flat side of the cone on palm and twist palms together in a round movement to compress dough into a thick flat blob (pedha).

9. Dust with flour and roll out the blob again to an 8 inch diameter disc. Refrigerate for an hour on butter paper.

10. Heat griddle and shallow fry both sides over low heat till golden.

Tips

Time
Preparation: 1½ hours
Cooking: 8-9 minutes for each paratha.

To serve
Serve with chicken kurchan or tala gosht. For recipes see pp. 5 and 25

SERVES: 4

SHEERMAL

A dough made of almost equal quantities of flour, milk and clarified butter (ghee) makes this a delicious and rich bread.

Ingredients

Flour	17 oz/2 cups	Salt to taste	
Milk	14 fl oz/1¾ cups	Sugar	¼ oz/1 tsp
Clarified butter (ghee)	8¾ oz/1 cup	Vetiver (kewda)	2 drops
Flour to dust pan		White butter for brushing	
Saffron	a pinch		

Method

1. Sift flour with salt onto a kneading platter.
2. Dissolve saffron in ¾ fl oz milk. Keep aside.
3. Heat the remaining milk and dissolve sugar in it. Cool and add vetiver.
4. Make a well in the flour and pour in the milk and sugar mixture. Gradually mix flour and milk and knead to a soft dough. Cover with wet cloth and set aside for 10 minutes.
5. Melt the clarified butter. Knead the dough again, adding small quantities of the butter till it is all used up.
6. Divide the dough into 12 equal balls. Cover and keep aside for 10 minutes.
7. Using a rolling pin roll out balls into 8 inch, round discs.
8. Prick all over with a fork. Arrange on a greased baking tray and bake in a preheated oven at 350 °F for 4 minutes.
9. Bring out and brush with saffron. Bake again for 4 minutes.

Time

Preparation: 1¼ hours
Cooking: 8-10 minutes for each batch.

To Serve

Brush sheermal with white butter and serve immediately

TANDOORI ROTI

A popular unleavened, wholewheat flour bread, baked in cylindrical clay ovens or the tandoor. It is the staple of most of rural North India.

Ingredients

Wholewheat flour   17 oz/2 cups
Clarified butter (*ghee*) to grease baking tray

Flour to dust
Salt to taste

Method

1. Sieve the flour with the salt onto a kneading platter.

2. Make a well in the flour and pour approximately 12 fl oz/1½ cups water into it. Gradually mix the flour and water and then knead to a soft dough.

3. Cover with a damp cloth and set aside for 20 minutes.

4. Divide into 8 portions. Make into balls and dust with flour.

5. Pat and flatten each ball with the palms to make 6 inch wide discs.

6. Wearing an oven glove stick the roti to the side of a moderately hot tandoor. Bake for two minutes then peal off swiftly. Place on a greased baking tray and bake for 5 to 6 minutes at 350 °F in a preheated oven.

Tips

Time
Preparation: 30 minutes
Cooking: 7 minutes for each roti

To Serve
Serve with any curry

SERVES: 4

NAAN

A light, leavened bread that can be made rich
by applying butter when ready.

Ingredients

Flour	17 oz/2 cups		Nigella (*kalonji*) seeds	¼ oz/1 tsp	
Baking powder	¼ oz/1 tsp		Salt to taste		
Clarified butter (*ghee*) to grease tray			Soda bi-carb	a pinch	
Flour to dust			Sugar	¼ oz/1 tsp	
Groundnut/peanut oil	1 fl oz/2 tbs		White butter	1 oz/2 tbs	
Melon (*magaz*) seeds	¼ oz/1 tsp		Yoghurt	1 oz/2 tbs	
Milk	1½ fl oz/3 tbs				

Method

1. Sift flour, salt, soda bi-carb and baking powder onto a kneading platter.
2. Whip sugar, yoghurt and milk together.
3. Make a well in the flour, pour 8 fl oz/ 1 cup water and the milk, sugar and yoghurt mixture. Mix well. Knead to make a dough.
4. Cover with moist cloth and keep aside for 10 minutes.
5. Add oil and knead again to make the dough absorb the oil.
6. Cover with moist cloth and keep aside for 2 hours, till dough rises.
7. Divide the dough into 6 balls. Flatten balls and sprinkle nigella and melon seeds. Cover and set aside for 5 minutes.
8. Roll and flatten each ball between your palms. Stretch dough to one side to give the naan an elongated shape.
9. Using oven gloves or a cushion pad stick the naan inside a moderately hot tandoor for 3 minutes. Alternatively, place the naan on a greased tray and bake in an oven for 10 minutes at 375 °F.

Time

Preparation: 2½ hours
Cooking: 15 minutes each

To Serve

Apply butter, if desired, and serve immediately